# Journey to SonRise

## Lent Devotional *Prayer* Journal

# Journey to SonRise

## Lent Devotional *Prayer* Journal

---

Joy L. Wilkerson

*Journey to SonRise: Lent Devotional Prayer Journal*
Copyright © February 2018 by Joy L. Wilkerson

Scripture quotations unless otherwise noted are taken from the Holy Bible, New Living Translation, copyright © 1996, 2004, 2007 by Tyndale House Foundation. Used by permission of Tyndale House Publishers, Inc., Carol Stream, Illinois 60188. All rights reserved.

Scripture quotations marked NKJV are taken from the New King James Version®. Copyright © 1982 by Thomas Nelson. Used by permission. All rights reserved.

Scripture quotations marked KJV are taken from the King James Version. Public Domain

ISBN 978-1-982-00082-0

Printed in the United States of America

## Dedication

I give God all the glory for the people He has placed in my life who have graced my growth, spirit, soul and body. For this I give God praise!

# Introduction

*In both the Jewish and Christian tradition, the number 40 has symbolic meaning. A period of 40 days or years, more than being a literal measurement, represents a long time and a period of preparation or testing. When the 40 days or years have passed, the appropriate period or "right amount of time" has been completed in preparation for the working of God's grace* (from Busted Halo, March 10, 2017 by Neela Kale). In the New Testament Gospels of Matthew, Mark and Luke, the Lord fasted for 40 days and nights in preparation for the beginning of His public ministry.

The season of Lent is the 40 day period between Ash Wednesday and Easter Sunday, excluding Sundays. Sundays are not counted as they are celebratory days for worship. Lent lasts 40 days so that we will spend the "right amount of time" in this period of preparation before Easter. The number 40 is symbolic more than a specific count of the days in Lent.

Prepare to reflect, renew and (re)commit to the things of Christ as we *Journey to SonRise* together. As you **reflect** on the daily devotions, **renew** yourself with the daily prayers and **(re)commit** to live a life as exampled by our Lord Jesus Christ, you will be spiritually equipped for the journey.

# Ash Wednesday
## First Day of Lent

**Have mercy on me, O God, because of your unfailing love. Because of your great compassion, blot out the stain of my sins. Wash me clean from my guilt. Purify me from my sin.**
**Psalm 51:1-2**

We have all sinned and fallen short of the glory of God. One of the biggest causes of our falling short is distractions. We allow the things of the world to distract us and take our focus from God. It was only a few weeks ago that we were committing to do better than we had in the previous year. We were going to eat healthier and exercise more. We were going to be fiscally responsible and save money by taking our lunch and cooking dinner at home. We were going to stop drinking, cursing and fussing. We were going to be on time and the list goes on. Our intentions were good but we were not intentional about committing to the goals that we set.

At some point we simply stopped doing what we said we would. One reason may be that the goals we set were not God-inspired but people inspired. Maybe we wanted a better physique, not so we could be fit to do kingdom work but so we could catch a mate in the coming year.

As we embark on the season of Lent, it causes us to take pause once again and reflect on just how far we have fallen. If the practice in your faith is to have an Ash Wednesday service, after listening to the homily, you become introspective as you come to receive the imposition of ashes in the sign of the cross across your forehead.

Often at Lent, when we think about the sacrifice Jesus made, it causes our convictions and commitments to be even stronger than they were at the beginning of the year. But Jesus is calling us to walk in his will and way year round. We are not called to be more holy during Eastertide than at the start of a New Year or any other time. We all struggle in certain areas but God is able to create in us a new heart if we choose to be intentional about pleasing him and not impressing people. Don't stop striving. Every time you fall short, recommit to starting anew trusting that God is right there with you.

***

**Prayer:** *Lord wash me clean from my guilt. Purify me today from my sins. Do not allow me to lose focus of the plan that you have for my life. Make me to know your wisdom and guide me in the areas where I struggle so I can be more like you. Today I (re) commit to* _____

_____

_____. Amen.

**But you desire honesty from the womb, teaching me wisdom even there. Purify me from my sins, and I will be clean; wash me, and I will be whiter than snow.**
**Psalm 51:6-7**

As we journey toward SonRise, truth telling is sometimes difficult. It is difficult to be truthful to others when we cannot be honest with ourselves. We know what we should do and say but we often do not follow through. We rationalize why we didn't do this or that or we tell ourselves we will follow through the next day. But many times we are simply in denial. We are afraid to do what You are calling us to do or we are simply being stubborn.

Lord you desire honesty. You taught us this from the womb so it may dwell in our hearts. Father, with the wisdom that you have poured into me let me speak truth to power for your glory. You have not given me a spirit of fear but of power, love and a sound mind. As I rest in you, I can be honest in all situations. I can stand firm on your Word trusting you to back me up. As you answer the questions in my spirit, I move forward knowing the battle is already won. Thank you God, for preparing me with wisdom in the womb to choose your Son as my Savior.

***

**Prayer:** *On today Lord – I ask that you purify me from my sin. When you clean me – I will be fully clean and willing to tell the truth to myself and to others. I want to be a living testimony for you. As I speak truth to others, let me speak in love. Guide me with not only the words to say, but how and when to say them. Let them be beneficial and uplifting to the hearer. As I speak to _____ touch their hearts to receive in love. On today I_____*

_____

_____

_____

_____

_____Amen.

# Day 3 of Lent

_____ 20 ____

## Open my eyes to see
## the wonderful truths in your instructions.
## Psalm 119:18

As we continue to take this journey toward SonRise and are introspective, we are faced with looking in the mirror and asking, "Who do I really see?" We are called to look beyond the physical and do some soul-searching about the kind of person we are. Are we a good representative of Jesus Christ? Are we following his instructions?

God's Word is filled with instructions on how to live. His Word guides us in the world like a lamp guides us in the darkness. Often we are misled in the world because we think we see and know what is going on and therefore have control. Yet when the truth of God's word is revealed, you realize there is only one Sovereign God and his commands are ours to follow.

*** 

**Prayer:** *Gracious Creator God, open my eyes to see the wonderful truths in your instructions. When the world would try to distract and deceive, make your pathway clear. Lord guide me to follow your instructions particularly in the areas of _____*

_____

_____

_____

_____.

_I commit to study your Word daily so it will be in my heart and I will readily recognize your voice from the competing voices in the world. Your Word is the way, the truth and the life. So guide me with your Word while I run this race so that I am not running in vain._ Amen.

# Day 4 of Lent
## _____ 20 ____

**Your word is a lamp to guide my feet
and a light for my path.
Psalm 119:105**

Light, the Light (God the Father, the Bright and Morning Star) provides clarity. When you try to operate in darkness you are confused. You cannot see where you are going so you are trying to feel your way around. If you are in familiar territory, you may be able to make it for a short distance in the dark. If you wake up in the middle of the night and have to go to the bathroom, you can probably get there and back without turning on a light. But when you start trying to do too much for too long in the dark, it just doesn't turn out right.

God is calling us to *walk in the Light*. Just like we operate better when we can physically see in the day time or when we turn lights on at night, we operate better spiritually when our lights are turned on in our minds. And we do that by studying and meditating on God's Word. In the past, I didn't understand a lot of what I was reading because I was doing simply that...just reading. I was not MEDITATING on God's Word. When you "meditate" you seek true understanding. You ask the questions, "What does what I read mean to me?" "How can I apply it in my life?"

***

**Prayer:** *Father, as I study your Word, guide and direct me to ask the right questions so I know the right way to go on life's journey. Let it be clear if I should go left or if I should go right. Let me wake up singing "walk in the light, beautiful light, come where the dewdrops of mercy shine bright. Oh shine all around us by day and by night, Jesus the light of the world". Guide my feet in these areas _____*

_____

_____

_____

_____

*_____ so I will be a better disciple for you.* Amen.

# First Sunday in Lent

_____ 20 ____

## Psalm 25:1-10

*O Lord, I give my life to you. I trust in you, my God! Do not let me be disgraced, or let my enemies rejoice in my defeat. No one who trusts in you will ever be disgraced, but disgrace comes to those who try to deceive others.*

*Show me the right path, O Lord; point out the road for me to follow. Lead me by your truth and teach me, for you are the God who saves me. All day long I put my hope in you. Remember, O Lord, your compassion and unfailing love, which you have shown from long ages past. Do not remember the rebellious sins of my youth. Remember me in the light of your unfailing love, for you are merciful, O Lord.*

*The Lord is good and does what is right; he shows the proper path to those who go astray. He leads the humble in doing right, teaching them his way. The Lord leads with unfailing love and faithfulness all who keep his covenant and obey his demands.*

**I praise God for what he has promised.**
**I trust in God, so why should I be afraid?**
**What can mere mortals do to me?**
**Psalm 56:4**

Earlier in the year, I heard a sermon that said, "God is getting ready to do something that your vocabulary cannot explain". Those were words of expectation and promise. While they are exciting to hear, they can also produce anxiety. Although we ask God for more, the unknown brings nervousness and sometimes fear. But if we trust God, why should we be afraid? God has not given us the spirit of fear but of power, love and a sound mind. What can humans do to us if we have God on our side? If the Lord said it, then it is so.

Jesus in his humanity was anxious but he said Father, let your will be done. Despite the thorns on his head and the nails in his hands and feet, Jesus trusted his Father. What could the Romans do to him except nail him to a cross? All power was in God's hands and he rose Jesus up again with that power. I praise God for Jesus. I praise God for what he has promised.

\*\*\*

**Prayer:** *Most gracious heavenly Father, thank you for your promise. Thank you for your Son. When I think about what*

16

*he did and how he trusted you, it gives me strength and courage to trust you. What can men and women do to me? So I will not fear. You have not given me the spirit of fear, but of power, love and a sound mind. I will be bold and step out and do what you are calling me to do. I will stop procrastinating regarding _____*

_____

_____

_____

_____.

*Thank you Lord in advance for blowing my mind because I trusted you to fulfill the promise you made.* Amen.

# Day 6 of Lent

## _____ 20 ____

## Teach us to realize the brevity of life, so that we may grow in wisdom.
## Psalm 90:12

The NJKV says "teach us to number our days" and if you have marked a milestone birthday, studied for final exams, gotten married, or had a baby, then you've "numbered your days". You may not have called it that but you knew exactly how many days you had left until the big event. God is teaching us to live every day with the kind of clarity we get when we are under a deadline. When you are close to a deadline, you don't lounge on the couch all day watching TV You have higher priority things to do.

When Jesus came to earth, he knew his time was limited. His priority was fulfilling his Father's business. As he cried out to his Father in the garden of Gethsemane "not my will but yours be done", he knew his time was drawing near. As he hung on the cross on Calvary's hill, he was not numbering the days, but he was counting down the hours; the minutes. He knew exactly how much time he had and used the wisdom of his heavenly Father to make every moment count.

We do not know exactly how much time we have but we do know our time on earth is limited. When you know your time is limited, it forces you to limit what you do with your time. It is about prioritizing the people and tasks that matter most. When we recognize *the brevity of life*, it causes us to grow in wisdom regarding what, or more importantly who is worth our limited time. We hope to live a longtime but we know not the hour that we will fly away. So let us make today and every day count by running all the demands for our time through a filter and focusing on what or who truly matter the most.

***

**Prayer:** *Most gracious God, teach me to number my days. Teach me to focus on those who matter most in my life. Let me practice love and forgiveness. Let me leave the past in the past and live in the present because the future is not promised. Today, I (re) commit to* _____

_____

_____

_____

_____ *because*
*I know not the day nor the hour that I will fly away.* Amen.

_____ 20 ____

**Shout joyful praises to God, all the earth!**
**Sing about the glory of his name!**
**Tell the world how glorious he is.**
**Psalm 66:1-2**

My desire is to hear my Father say, "My beloved child, you bring me great joy". The joy of the Lord is my strength and as I aim for joy in my life, I have to express joy. I have to shout joyful praises to God. I have to sing and shout about the glory of his name. I am called to sing and dance in worship and praise. I just cannot stop praising his name and telling the world how glorious he is. I was created to praise the Lord.

I am excited to sing God's praises for all that he has done for me. Despite my situation or circumstance, I begin my day with joy. Joy sings in me and I cannot help but share it wherever I go. In God's presence is fullness of joy. I am thankful to be in God's presence.

\*\*\*

**Prayer:** *Almighty God, you are glorious! The Word says let everything that has breath praise the Lord. I thank you for breath in my body and I ask that you continue to keep me healthy and strong so I can continue to praise your Holy name. I thank you for _____*

_____

_____.

*Despite my situation or circumstance, let me always remember that this joy that I have, the world did not give it to me and the world cannot take it away. Amen!*

# Day 8 of Lent

_____ 20 ____

**But let all who take refuge in you rejoice; let them sing joyful praises forever. Spread your protection over them, that all who love your name may be filled with joy.**
**Psalm 5:11**

Despite trying times in our relationships, because we take refuge in you we can rejoice. We are not perfect so we should not expect those whom we love and care about to be perfect. When you think about the things they do to get on your nerves, imagine what you do to get on their nerves. Do not be so quick to let relationships go because God was not so quick to let our relationship with him go. God sent his Son to earth to live among us so he could understand everything we go through. Jesus never faltered but he always understood.

Jesus came that we might have abundant life. Jesus came that we might have joy and that our joy would be complete through the sacrifice of his life for us. That is love, true love. If Jesus can love us despite all our sins, surely we can love one another despite our idiosyncrasies. That sounds a little bit like idio(t)-sin-crazies. Well it means an odd way of thinking or behaving, so that sounds about right. But hey, not one of us is perfect yet we serve a perfect Savior so let us aim for joy as we strive to love one another as Jesus loves us.

\*\*\*

**Prayer:** *Lord, I take refuge in you today and every day. I sing praises to you forever. Spread your protection over me and those whom I love. I love your name so fill me with joy. Let all who love your name be filled with joy and that our joy may be complete in you. Lord give me the patience to deal with* _____ *understanding that I am not perfect either and it takes compromise and understanding for relationships to work. I strive to be more like you Jesus and I (re) commit to*_____

_____

_____

_____

_____

_____

_____Amen.

**The LORD is my shepherd; I have all that I need.
He lets me rest in green meadows;
he leads me beside peaceful streams.
Psalm 23:1-2**

We all need breathing room. It comes when we are intentional about slowing down. We cannot keep moving at a record breaking pace trying to do everything for everybody. We cannot burn the candle at both ends trying to achieve our career goals to the detriment of our health or our family. We have to stop and reprioritize our life.

Jesus was no doubt the busiest man that ever walked the earth. Yet he never hurried anywhere. He allowed people to stop him. People followed him when he went to pray, but he found solitude. He spent time with his Father for guidance. He rested so he could effectively attend to the needs of the people. Are you greater than the Master? Allow yourself some breathing room today.

\*\*\*

**Prayer:** *Jehovah-Rohi, thank you for allowing me to rest and experience peace. You provide everything I need. Your Son led a productive but simple life. Guide me to do the same. Today I remove _____ from my to-do list and allow myself breathing room to spend with you.* Amen.

## Joyful are those who obey his laws and search for him with all their hearts.
### Psalm 119:2

The season of Lent leads us to search our hearts. We think about things we committed to do or stop doing at the beginning of the year and now we find that we are not making much progress. It is easy to become discouraged when life is providing daily challenges with family, finances and health. We may ask ourselves, "What is the point of trying to do right?" Those living their own way seem to be doing as well or better than me.

Do not let appearances fool you. The grass is not greener on the other side. *Joyful are those who obey God's laws.* You have to search for him with all your heart while he may be found. Despite the mockers and scorners, Jesus stayed the course. Joy is a fruit of the spirit not based on situation or circumstance. If you stay the course by obeying God's Word, you will experience his joy.

\*\*\*

**Prayer:** *Lord, you bring me so much joy. Early will I search for you with all my heart. Put in me a desire to consistently study your Word. I especially need help in the area of* _____. *Guide me to scripture that will encourage me to press on.* Amen.

# Second Sunday in Lent

_____ 20 _____

## Psalm 22:23-31

*Praise the L*ORD*, all you who fear him! Honor him, all you descendants of Jacob! Show him reverence, all you descendants of Israel! For he has not ignored or belittled the suffering of the needy. He has not turned his back on them, but has listened to their cries for help.*

*I will praise you in the great assembly. I will fulfill my vows in the presence of those who worship you. The poor will eat and be satisfied. All who seek the L*ORD *will praise him. Their hearts will rejoice with everlasting joy. The whole earth will acknowledge the L*ORD *and return to him. All the families of the nations will bow down before him. For royal power belongs to the L*ORD*. He rules all the nations.*

*Let the rich of the earth feast and worship. Bow before him, all who are mortal, all whose lives will end as dust. Our children will also serve him. Future generations will hear about the wonders of the Lord. His righteous acts will be told to those not yet born. They will hear about everything he has done.*

**Send out your light and your truth; let them guide me. Let them lead me to your holy mountain, to the place where you live.**
**Psalm 43:3**

Distractions run rampant in our lives. There are multiple things vying for our attention. Today with all the technology and social media, it is difficult for us humans to communicate with each other one on one and face to face. You can only imagine how difficult it is for us to take time out for you. But Jesus demonstrated time and again the importance of drawing away in prayer.

Today I strive to take time away from the demands of the world and have a little talk with your darling Son Jesus if only to thank him for the sacrifice that he made for me. A little talk with Jesus makes everything alright.

\*\*\*

**Prayer:** *Lord thank you for sending your Chosen One to guide me. As I bow at your altar Lord, I recognize you as the source of all my joy and I will praise you with all my heart, my God. When I begin to stray, guide me back to your holy mountain, the place where you live. Take my mind off of* _____

_____*and let it be stayed* on you. Keep me focused on you Father. Amen.

# Day 12 of Lent

_____ 20 ____

**I entrust my spirit into your hand.
Rescue me, LORD, for you are a faithful God.
Psalm 31:5**

Lord, I don't always do what I say I am going to do. A decision I made yesterday, like not going to bed as scheduled, impacts the present moment. Yet, I trust you Lord to guide me to do better. Each day's experience provides opportunities to develop new skills and a deeper understanding of all that I am capable of being and doing. I have no need to cling to the past or fear the future because something greater is unfolding in me now.

Greater is coming because your Son Jesus gave his life for me. As Jesus entrusted his Spirit into your hand, I entrust my spirit into yours. You are a faithful God and I trust you to rescue me from doing it my way.

\*\*\*

**Prayer:** *Merciful God, as I let go, I ask that you take hold. As I let go and let God, I hold to your unchanging hand and build my hopes on things eternal. Today I relinquish control of* _____

_____

_____. Amen.

# Day 13 of Lent

## _____ 20 _____

**You have given me your shield of victory. Your right hand supports me; your help has made me great.**
**Psalm 18:35**

When the enemy comes to distract you from doing God's work respond like Nehemiah. Say, "I am engaged in a great work, so I can't come. Why should I stop working to come and meet with you?" The Lord will support your efforts and give you the victory if you stay focused on him and completing the great work he has called you to do.

Jesus knew the great work he came to earth to do. He focused on it from day one and did not stop until it was finished. Stop trying to be everything to everybody. Stop trying to please everybody. If you focus on your Father's business, everything else will fall in place. Allow God's right hand to support you and make you great.

\*\*\*

**Prayer:** *Holy God, thank you for giving me a shield of victory. When I am tempted to be distracted by all the options available to use up my time, remind me of the great work you have for me to do. Lord, I will stay focused on* _____

_____. *With the support of your right hand, I will not stop until the assignment you have given me is finished. In Jesus name.* Amen.

_____ 20 _____

## Create in me a clean heart, O God; and renew a right spirit within me.
### Psalm 51:10 KJV

Psalm 51 is one of the most well-known prayers of King David. He prayed this after he was convicted in spirit regarding his adulterous relationship. He is asking God to create a clean heart and renew a right spirit within him. What has convicted your spirit today? What has the Nathan in your life shared with you causing you to turn your head to the Lord in prayer seeking forgiveness?

Prayer is a disciplined decision. We are called to be serious and watchful in our prayers. Prayer and intercession take us into the counsel of the Lord. There are some things that only come by prayer *and* fasting. Fasting is not something to be done only during Lent for form or fashion. Prayer and fasting is a necessity to break yokes and allow us to walk holy before the Lord. Jesus taught us how to pray. Let us follow his lead.

\*\*\*

**Prayer:** *Lord, renew a right spirit within me. Allow me to be a positive example to those around me. Guide me in fasting so I will be empowered to make wise decisions in the area(s) of* _____

_____ *where I struggle most.* Amen.

_____ 20 ____

**Lift your hands toward the sanctuary,
and praise the LORD.
Psalm 134:2**

Friday represents the beginning of the weekend for a lot of people. If you are a student or a teacher, it is generally the last day of class. If you work, it is generally the last day of the work week. Of course there are exceptions. Some schools offer classes on Saturday. Retail businesses are open six and seven days a week. But even still, most people "live" for the weekend. Everything that we do (or don't do) Monday through Friday is so we can enjoy the weekend.

God wants us to have an abundant life every day and not just on the weekend or our day off. Every day that we wake up is an opportunity to praise God's name. Find something to look forward to everyday and not just Friday. Jesus paid it all so we can lift our hands in praise every day. There is something to be thankful for each and every day. Don't just "live" for the weekend but live for Christ.

\*\*\*

**Prayer:** *Father, open my eyes to the fact that the sanctuary is not just a physical building but it is wherever you are* *present. Let your presence enfold me and allow me to freely praise your holy name. From the rising of the sun to the setting of the same, your name is worthy to be praised. I commit to engaging in a full life every day and not just on the weekends. I will take time to* _____

_____

_____

_____ *whenever the Spirit leads me and not just on special occasions. Life is too short to hold back my praise. Today, I lift my hands toward the sanctuary in praise to you.* Amen.

# Day 16 of Lent

## _____ 20 _____

**I will lift up my eyes to the hills—From whence comes my help? My help *comes* from the LORD, Who made heaven and earth. Psalm 121:1 NKJV**

Tasha Cobbs Leonard has a song called "Forever At Your Feet" on her *Heart, Passion, Pursuit* CD. The song opens saying, "I'll be seated at your feet, to worship at your feet...forever". That is an excellent place to be. The Lord simply wants us to worship and adore him; to praise him. At his feet is where he wants us. But sometimes we are challenged to worship him because we have left our position at his feet.

We have forgotten from where our help comes because we have been relying on our own strength too long. Our help comes from the Lord who made heaven and earth. Jesus did not forget where his help came from. Up until his very last fleshly moment, he relied on his help as he commended his spirit to his Father. Stay in position at the feet of Jesus. Constantly look to the hills from which your help comes.

\*\*\*

**Prayer:** *Lord, let me always remember to look to the hills. Remind me to keep my eyes focused on you because from you is where all my help comes. You are the Source of my* strength; the Source of everything. If I stay at your feet, you will guide me in the way that I should go. I commit to stop operating in my own strength regarding _____

_____

_____

_____and turn it over to you. Amen.

# Third Sunday in Lent

_____ 20 _____

## Psalm 19

*The heavens proclaim the glory of God. The skies display his craftsmanship. Day after day they continue to speak; night after night they make him known. They speak without a sound or word; their voice is never heard. Yet their message has gone throughout the earth, and their words to all the world.*

*God has made a home in the heavens for the sun. It bursts forth like a radiant bridegroom after his wedding. It rejoices like a great athlete eager to run the race. The sun rises at one end of the heavens and follows its course to the other end. Nothing can hide from its heat.*

*The instructions of the LORD are perfect, reviving the soul. The decrees of the LORD are trustworthy, making wise the simple. The commandments of the LORD are right, bringing joy to the heart. The commands of the LORD are clear, giving insight for living. Reverence for the LORD is pure, lasting forever.*

*The laws of the Lord are true; each one is fair. They are more desirable than gold, even the finest gold. They are sweeter than honey, even honey dripping from the comb. They are a warning to your servant, a great reward for those who obey them.*

*How can I know all the sins lurking in my heart? Cleanse me from these hidden faults. Keep your servant from deliberate sins! Don't let them control me. Then I will be free of guilt and innocent of great sin.*

*May the words of my mouth and the meditation of my heart be pleasing to you, O Lord, my rock and my redeemer.*

### I stay awake through the night,
### thinking about your promise.
### Psalm 119:148

Rest is important. God tells us we can sleep in peace because he never slumbers or sleeps. Yet I often find myself awake in the early morning hours. The sun has not come up so it still seems like the night. Often waking up in the middle of the "night" is due to negative stress or worry. But every now and then it is caused by excitement or what I call positive stress.

When you are on a specific assignment for the Lord, for a short season, he enables you to get by on a limited number of hours of sleep. I imagine this is how Jesus felt in his final days. Before I get up, I lay in bed meditating on God's promises. As I arise each day to fulfill my kingdom assignment, I thank the Lord for *such a time as this* and move forward to carry out my purpose.

*** 

**Prayer:** *Adonai, I thank you for not slumbering. I thank you for giving me the exact amount of rest needed in order to be refreshed to joyfully join you in your work. Guide me to stay on task to fulfill my assignment of _____ _____ so the promises of your Word might be fulfilled.* Amen.

_____ 20 ____

**The LORD *is* my light and my salvation; Whom shall I fear?**
**The LORD *is* the strength of my life;**
**Of whom shall I be afraid?**
**Psalm 27:1**

*Lord I set my hope on you; I set my hope on your love. I set my hope on you, the everlasting God.* You are my light and my salvation so there is no reason to fear. You are my Strong Tower in which I can run. So there is no reason to be afraid. I trust you Lord with my life.

Jesus trusted God with his life. He knew that he would return to sit in heaven. Because Jesus came to earth to dwell with us and is now sitting in heaven watching over us, I can trust you Lord until it is my time to see you in paradise. Until then I will worship you daily.

***

**Prayer:** *Everlasting God, you are my light and my salvation. You are the strength of my life. I will fear no one or nothing. I will keep on trusting in you until I die. You did not create me to worry or fear so I will step out boldly today and begin* _____

_____

_____.

*I will remain confident in this, I will see the goodness of the Lord. It is so, in Jesus name.* Amen.

**And let the beauty of the LORD our God be upon us, And establish the work of our hands for us; Yes, establish the work of our hands.**
**Psalm 90:17 NKJV**

Most of us are familiar with the story of Mary and Martha when Jesus came to visit. *Martha was distracted with much serving but Mary chose the good part* of sitting at Jesus' feet. Martha started out aiming to please Jesus but she got caught up in self-service. She wanted recognition for the work she was doing instead of doing the work to bring glory to God.

We have been there; serving as a committee chairperson or leading a project at work. We wanted things to be perfect but at some point the focus moved from things being the best for the organization's benefit, to you being recognized as the best for the work you were doing. Ask God to establish the work of your hands for the kingdom. Remember, it is not about you.

\*\*\*

**Prayer:** *Lord, I am your servant. As I serve, let the only approval I seek be yours. If I do the work you are calling me to do in the area of _____, your people will be blessed and you will pleased.* Amen.

**The one thing I ask of the LORD—the thing I seek most—
is to live in the house of the LORD all the days of my life,
delighting in the LORD's perfections and
meditating in his Temple.
Psalm 27:4**

Most of us consider the house of the Lord as a physical building where we go to worship corporately with others. But our bodies are God's temple and the Holy Spirit dwells in us. So when you read the above text it should take you to another level. It should make you want to sing, "Lord prepare me to be a living sanctuary for you".

Jesus was both fully human and fully Divine. He had the optimal experience of dwelling in the temple and being the Temple that dwells in us. Let us strive to live a life dedicated only to pleasing God; recognizing that our bodies are not our own.

\*\*\*

**Prayer:** *Holy Spirit, continuously stir up my spirit to want to live holy for you. In you I live, and move, and have my very being. I delight in your Word and I will meditate on it day and night. Direct me to specific scriptures related to _____*

_____

*so I may grow stronger in those areas. My desire is to grow closer to you. It is so, in Jesus name.* Amen.

***

*Reflections at the halfway point...*

# Day 21 of Lent

_____ 20 ____

**You light a lamp for me.**
**The LORD, my God, lights up my darkness.**
**Psalm 18:28**

I, like many, seem to work best against tight deadlines. However, this is not the best way to work. It increases stress and leaves no room for the unexpected. Fortunately, while working on this devotional, the Lord provided some breathing room. He *lit a lamp* and *lit up my darkness*.

I planned to write forty-seven devotions, one for each day of Lent and one for each Sunday. Due to procrastination, I needed to write five devotions a day to meet my deadline. During my meditation time, the Lord revealed to only write forty devotions for the days of Lent and insert scripture on the Sundays. This saved me a day and a half of writing. The Lord also allowed Mother Nature to intervene with a snow day during the writing process. When the Lord provides light, use it wisely.

***

**Prayer:** *Lord, thank you for your marvelous light. As I meditate on your Word and spend time in prayer, let me use the wise counsel you provide, especially in the area of* _____ *so that I can give you all the honor and praise due your Holy name.* Amen.

42

## Day 22 of Lent

_____ 20 _____

**For they are transplanted to the LORD's own house.
They flourish in the courts of our God.
Psalm 92:13**

The word transplant means to move or relocate. The text refers to the godly flourishing like palm trees and growing strong like the cedars of Lebanon. Often plants have to be replanted in different pots with fresh soil to produce at maximum capacity. As I began working on this journal I repositioned myself. I moved from sitting in a chair facing the T.V. to a chair facing the window where I could look outside and see nature.

Jesus repositioned himself. He was transplanted from heaven to earth to show us the way. He came to earth to operate at maximum capacity for his Father. In order for us to flourish, Jesus came to earth incarnate to understand our walk but without falling. Let us follow Jesus' example and flourish in the courts of our God.

\*\*\*

**Prayer:** *Lord, I thank you for a place to worship your Holy name with other believers. A day in your courts is better than a thousand. On the days when I am inclined to sleep in or _____ remind me of your goodness and encourage me to come flourish in the house of the Lord.* Amen.

## Fourth Sunday in Lent

_____ 20 ____

### Psalm 107:1-3, 17-22

*Give thanks to the LORD, for he is good! His faithful love endures forever. Has the LORD redeemed you? Then speak out! Tell others he has redeemed you from your enemies. For he has gathered the exiles from many lands, from east and west, from north and south.*

*Some were fools; they rebelled and suffered for their sins. They couldn't stand the thought of food, and they were knocking on death's door.*

*"LORD, help!" they cried in their trouble, and he saved them from their distress. He sent out his word and healed them, snatching them from the door of death.*

*Let them praise the LORD for his great love and for the wonderful things he has done for them. Let them offer sacrifices of thanksgiving and sing joyfully about his glorious acts.*

# Day 23 of Lent

_____ 20 ____

## Those who love your instructions
## have great peace and do not stumble.
## Psalm 119:165

Today I was afforded a day off work without having to use vacation time. Like many, I have a hectic schedule but if I am honest, a lot of the hectic is self-induced. Most of us have a lot of "hurry and stress" that God did not design. He has a promise and plan for our lives described in his Word. All we need to do is follow it.

Jesus followed his Father's plan to the final detail. He was not rushed but he was never late. He listened to his Father's instructions and had great peace and did not stumble. He was righteously indignant every now and then, but never truly stressed because the Master Teacher was a star pupil. Follow Jesus' example. Love and follow God's instructions and you will have great peace.

\*\*\*

**Prayer:** *Lord, I thank you for perfect peace when I keep my mind stayed on you. Guide me to keep your Word in my heart so I may live it daily. Today I eliminate stress and embrace peace by removing _____*

*_____ from my agenda and letting you have control In Jesus name.* Amen.

**He alone is my rock and my salvation,**
**my fortress where I will not be shaken.**
**Psalm 62:6**

One of my favorite CD's is from the movie <u>The Preacher's Wife</u>. One of my favorite songs on the CD is *I Go to the Rock*. Whitney Houston asks many questions: Where do I go; who do I talk to; who do I lean on when there is no foundation stable? The answer to every question is, "I go the Rock." God is the Rock and he is able to do anything but fail.

When the earth all around me is sinking sand, on Christ the solid rock I stand. Yes, God alone is my rock and my salvation. When I stand with God, I will not be shaken. God is always there when the storms of life are threatening, a refuge in time of trouble. I praise you God for being my rock.

***

**Prayer:** *Lord, I thank you for being my Rock. When all other ground is sinking sand, on Christ the Solid Rock I stand. Thank you Lord for being a firm foundation, guiding me as I go about my day. Lord, when I am faced with _____*

_____

*remind me that you are a refuge in a time of trouble. Give me the strength to stand firm on your Word.* Amen.

_____ 20 _____

**Sing a new song to the LORD, for he has done wonderful deeds. His right hand has won a mighty victory; his holy arm has shown his saving power!**
**Psalm 98:1**

The past few years have brought major storms and natural disasters throughout the nation and world. Tornadoes, hurricanes and fires have taken many lives. Survivors are mournful about both the family members they have lost and the loss of their life's possessions. In the midst of traumatic loss, God is still there with his holy arm outstretched showing his saving power.

During these times we can still give God a yet praise. Thinking about the wonderful deeds God has done causes you to sing a new song. Jesus was buried for three days but he rose with all power in his hands. He conquered hell and the grave so we could have the victory. That is something to sing about.

\*\*\*

**Prayer:** *Creator God, I give you praise for the wonderful deeds you have done in my life and the lives of those I love. Teach me to trust you, particularly in the area of _____*

_____.

*As I trust you, I obtain the victory through the saving power in your holy right arm.* Amen.

# Day 26 of Lent

_____ 20 _____

## Those who live in the shelter of the Most High will find rest in the shadow of the Almighty.
### Psalm 91:1

The best place to be is in the shadow of the Almighty. He will give you rest. The Word says to not grow weary in well doing. Often when we do good things, we feel we don't need to stop and take a break. But if we don't rest in the Savior's arms, our work will be in vain.

Every good thing we do is not a God-given task for us to do. Some things are meant for others to do but because they are not doing them when and how we think they should be done, we want to take over and do it ourselves. But when we operate out of turn in our own strength, God does not get the glory. Today, choose to live in the shelter of the Most High and let him give you rest.

***

**Prayer:** _Lord, guide my feet as I run this race because I don't want to run this race in vain. Show me my God-given task and let me do it well. Give me the patience and self-control to be still and allow others to do their God-given task without me trying to take over. Especially in the area of _____

_____ _teach me how to rest in the shadow of the Almighty and let others take the lead. In Jesus name._ Amen.

48

**I will praise you, LORD, with all my heart; I will tell of all the marvelous things you have done.**
**Psalm 9:1**

Our bodies unfortunately cannot tell the difference between positive stress and negative stress. When exciting, wonderful things are going on in our lives, we have a tendency to get anxious and giddy. We are looking forward to what is happening, but there is some trepidation regarding the unknown. How will things turn out? Can this be true? You may want to pinch yourself to make sure it is real.

Another idea is to praise the Lord with all your heart and share all the marvelous things that Jehovah Jireh has done. Trust God to take care of you in moments of uncertainty, good or bad. God is not a God of disorder, but of peace, so rest in his peace as you give him praise.

*** 

**Prayer:** *Adonai, My Great Lord, You are marvelous. I will share about your goodness wherever I go. I will praise you Lord with all my heart. As I look forward to* _____

_____ *I*

*ask that you calm my spirit for you have not given me the spirit of fear, but of power, love and a sound mind.* Amen.

## Day 28 of Lent

_____ 20 _____

**The very essence of your words is truth; all your just regulations will stand forever.**
**Psalm 119:160**

The Word of God is the truth. It is not just words about God; it is the Word of God. Times have changed but the inherent truth of God's Word is still relevant today. Don't neglect it. It is the foundation of a stable life. Read it and seek to understand how it applies to your daily life. It guides your walk. It feeds your faith.

Jesus taught us that we cannot live by bread alone but by every word that proceeds from the mouth of God. If Jesus knew the importance of living by God's Word, so should we. Dine on God's Word today. His just regulations will stand forever.

\*\*\*

**Prayer:** *Lord, thank you for your Word. As I read the scriptures allow me to see what it meant when it was written. More importantly, open my eyes and heart to the timeless truth behind what God is saying and how this truth applies to me today. I am especially seeking to grow in the area of _____*

_____.

*Please direct me to relevant texts in your Holy Word to strengthen me spiritually. In Jesus name.* Amen.

50

# Fifth Sunday in Lent

_____ 20 _____

## Psalm 119:9-16

*How can a young person stay pure?*
*By obeying your word.*
*I have tried hard to find you—*
*don't let me wander from your commands.*

*I have hidden your word in my heart,*
*that I might not sin against you.*
*I praise you, O LORD; teach me your decrees.*

*I have recited aloud*
*all the regulations you have given us.*
*I have rejoiced in your laws as much as in riches.*

*I will study your commandments*
*and reflect on your ways.*
*I will delight in your decrees*
*and not forget your word.*

**Day 29 of Lent**

_____ 20 ____

**Honor the LORD for the glory of his name.**
**Worship the LORD in the splendor of his holiness.**
**Psalm 29:2**

Honoring the Lord for the glory of his name and worshipping the Lord in the splendor of his holiness means putting God first. It means putting our wants and desires aside and seeking only his will for our lives. Shana Wilson has a song called *Give Me You*. She cries to the Lord, "Give me you, everything else can wait. Give me you; I hope I'm not too late".

Lord your timing is not our timing. I hope I am not too late. I seek to give you all the honor, glory and praise due your name. When I have you Lord, I have everything that I need. Your Word says seek first the kingdom of God and his righteous and all these things will be added. I trust your Word and believe you for your promises.

\*\*\*

**Prayer:** *Blessed Savior, you are worthy to be praised. From the rising of the sun, to the going down of the same, your name is worthy to be praised. I praise you for _____*

_____.

*Whenever I lose focus, remind me that everything revolves around you. Remind me, everything else can wait.* Amen.

**_____ 20 _____**

**Cast your cares on the Lord and he will sustain you; he will never let the righteous be shaken.**
**Psalm 55:22 NIV**

The tension in my neck is so tight. The pounding in my temple will not stop. What is really going on? I need a massage. Everything seems fine on the surface but there is a lot running around in my mind. But the Word says to cast my cares on the Lord and he will sustain me. He will never let the righteous be shaken.

His Son Jesus said in Matthew 11:29-30, *"Take my yoke upon you. Let me teach you, because I am humble and gentle at heart, and you will find rest for your souls. For my yoke is easy to bear, and the burden I give you is light."* Cast your cares on Jesus and he will give you rest. Let go and let God. It will sustain you better than a massage any day.

***

**Prayer:** *My Sustainer, I come casting my cares on you. Today I let go of seeking approval and acceptance from others. I let go of* _____

_____.

*Every heavy burden that I bear, I give to you and receive your light burden that is easy to bear.* Amen.

# Day 31 of Lent

_____ 20 ____

## Acknowledge that the LORD is God!
## He made us, and we are his.
## We are his people, the sheep of his pasture.
## Psalm 100:3

Lord, you are God. Lord you are good. When I think about all that is good, I thank God. Everything that you created, you said that it was good. You made me – I'm yours and I am good. Even with an unfavorable medical diagnosis or an unexpected change in life circumstances you are still good. Lord you have been better to me than I have been to myself.

You are my Shepherd and I am one of your sheep. Thank you for taking care of me. I appreciate your guidance. I appreciate your slowing me down even when I did not recognize or acknowledge that I needed it. Yes Lord, you are all God and you are all good.

***

**Prayer:** *Lord, you are good. I cannot praise you enough. You have been so good to me. You were especially good when* _____.
*As I remember, I can't help but give you praise. Teach me to give you, my great God, a great praise at all times. In Jesus name.* Amen.

_____ 20 _____

**Teach me to do your will, for you are my God. May your gracious Spirit lead me forward on a firm footing. Psalm 143:10**

Sometimes we think we are doing things right. Hindsight reveals that we are not. The Lord showed himself mighty in my life last year. So I was excited about the New Year and started making moves. They were good moves so I believed they were directed by God. Now I would have given the enemy credit if they were bad.

Well, how many of you know that everything good is not good for you, at least not right now? God is calling us to be still and know. When you cannot be still on your own, God will help you. Upcoming surgery caused me to slow down and realize now is not the time for some of these "good" things. If we stay in God's Word, he will teach us to do his will. Like Jesus in the garden of Gethsemane, not my will Lord but yours.

*** 

**Prayer:** *Lord, teach me to do your will, for you are my God. May your gracious Spirit lead me forward on firm footing especially in the area(s) of _____*

*_____.*

*Jesus Christ sent his Holy Spirit to guide us daily. Let me go in peace where the Spirit guides.* Amen.

# Day 33 of Lent

_____ 20 ____

**This is the day the LORD has made.
We will rejoice and be glad in it.
Psalm 118:24**

The Lord is Creator. Every day that unfolds is one made by the Master and we are called to be glad about it. The Lord is God, shining on us. Offer him a sacrifice of praise just for being God. Give thanks to the Lord, for he is good. His faithful love endures forever. Do not allow your pain to keep you from praising him. Do not allow your worries to keep you from worshipping him. Rejoice, I say rejoice!

Regardless of what you are going through – this is the day that the Lord has made. If you are here to see another day, tell the Lord thank you. If the Lord woke you up, there is still work left for you to do. Keep working until your God-given assignment is complete. Then you can be glad about it when you hear him say, "Well done!"

\*\*\*

**Prayer:** *Lord, this is a day that you have made and I am truly glad about it. I will enter into my _____ with thanksgiving in my heart. . As I complete each task of my assignment, I will do it with gladness in my heart. Thank you Lord for making this day. In Jesus name.* Amen.

**The LORD hears his people when they call to him for help.
He rescues them from all their troubles.
Psalm 34:17**

There have been times in my life when I climbed into bed and wept, crying out to God, just as you have. Such is life, especially when you decide to be transparent rather than protect some kind of "I'm altogether" image. In times like these it is comforting to know that God is able to handle it all. The Lord is full of compassion and mercy. *The Lord hears his people when they call to him for help. He rescues them from all their troubles.*

When you cry out to God he will respond but in order to hear your mind must be open to receive God's message. Allow the Lord to rescue you by removing the barriers of pride, fear and bitterness. Pride is thinking you can do it on your own. Fear is thinking God is not able to give you the ability to do it. Bitterness is not letting go which keeps you from getting on with your life. Position yourself to be rescued by removing the barriers.

\*\*\*

**Prayer:** *Lord, thank for hearing my cry for help. I especially need help to remove the barrier of _____ so I can move forward with my life and be all that you are calling me to be. Amen.*

# Palm Sunday

_____ 20 _____

## Psalm 118:1-2, 19-29

*Give thanks to the LORD, for he is good! His faithful love endures forever. Let all Israel repeat: His faithful love endures forever."*

*Open for me the gates where the righteous enter and I will go in and thank the LORD. These gates lead to the presence of the LORD, and the godly enter there.*
*I thank you for answering my prayer and giving me victory!*

*The stone that the builders rejected has now become the cornerstone. This is the LORD's doing, and it is wonderful to see. This is the day the LORD has made. We will rejoice and be glad in it. Please, LORD, please save us. Please, LORD, please give us success.*

*Bless the one who comes in the name of the LORD. We bless you from the house of the LORD. The LORD is God, shining upon us.  Take the sacrifice and bind it with cords on the altar. You are my God, and I will praise you! You are my God, and I will exalt you!*

*Give thanks to the LORD, for he is good!*
*His faithful love endures forever.*

_____ 20 _____

**Sin whispers to the wicked, deep within their hearts.
They have no fear of God at all.
Psalm 36:1-11**

When you reflect on Jesus having his last supper with his disciples, it makes you think of his betrayer, Judas. Judas was wicked – sin had to be whispering deep within his heart for him to betray Jesus. I mean, how could he go against the one he had been in companionship with for so long? The disciples were Jesus' closest friends, yet the closer he came to completing his earthly assignment, the farther away his friends drew.

Has there been a time in your life when sin was whispering deep within your heart? It was so deep it caused you to betray your closest friends and loved ones. Did you act like you had no fear of God? God is to be revered. His unfailing love is as vast as the heavens and his faithfulness reaches beyond the clouds. Those who do evil will fall. Choose God and keep from falling.

\*\*\*

**Prayer:** *Lord, forgive me for any evil I have done by word, thought, or deed. Guard my mind so when sin attempts to whisper in my heart, I will choose love. I choose love in my relationship(s) with _____*

*that I may not sin against you. Amen.*

# Day 36 of Lent ~ Holy Week
## _____ 20 _____

### But I will keep on hoping for your help;
### I will praise you more and more.
### Psalm 71:14

Jesus was in spiritual union with his disciples. During his three year ministry, he constantly provided the disciples help and prepared them for their future when he would no longer be with them. While they did not always follow his advice, the majority of the disciples continued to hope for his help even after they had messed up.

We are Jesus' modern day disciples. Despite our not following his advice or our mess ups, we still keep hoping for his help. We still desire his love. As Jesus continues to help us, we continue to praise him more and more. From the rising of the sun to the going down of the same he is worthy to be praised.

\*\*\*

**Prayer:** *Father God, thank you for being my rock and my fortress. I call on you today for help in the following areas:*

_____

_____.

*Guide me in the way in which I will go and I will praise you more and more. In the name of your darling Son Jesus. Amen.*

_____ 20 _____

**Please, God, rescue me! Come quickly, LORD, and help me. May those who try to kill me be humiliated and put to shame. May those who take delight in my trouble be turned back in disgrace.**
**Psalm 70 : 1-2**

As Jesus was praying in the Garden of Gethsemane, Judas came with a great multitude with swords and clubs. He came from the chief priests and elders of the people. Jesus could have cried at that moment for God to rescue him, but he knew all this was done so the Scriptures of the prophets might be fulfilled. Jesus remained silent because he knew the end of the story.

The end of the story was the beginning of eternal life for us. Because Jesus did not cry out for God to rescue but instead said, "thy will be done", we have a future. The Lord fights our battles giving us a future filled with hope. He provides a shield against those who take delight in my trouble.

***

**Prayer:** *Lord thank you for hearing me when I cry out for help. Teach me to trust you to fight my battles especially when it comes to* _____

_____

_____. *I trust You Lord. In Jesus name. Amen.*

# Day 38 of Lent ~ Maundy Thursday

## I will offer you a sacrifice of thanksgiving and call on the name of the Lᴏʀᴅ.
### Psalm 116:17

Jesus endured a lot for us on this mournful night. Even as he shared his last communion in the flesh with his disciples, he was being betrayed. Yet he continued to show and teach love as he washed the feet of his disciples. That is true love. Jesus continues to love us despite our actions and disobedience.

Even when we let Jesus down like Peter, he still keeps his promises to us. Jesus knows every action we will take before we even take it, yet he has an amazing plan for our life. All he wants is for us to say, "Yes, Lord!" We may be anxious at times but if we call on the name of the Lord he will see us through.

*** 

*Prayer: Lord, I thank you for enduring the ridiculing; the arrest and mock trial. I appreciate everything you endured on the night before you made the walk down Via Dolorosa headed toward Calvary's cross. You didn't have to but you did. I am especially thankful for* _____

_____.

*For it all I give you praise! In Jesus name. Amen.*

## Day 39 of Lent ~ Good Friday

_____ 20 _____

**My God, my God, why have you abandoned me?**
**Why are you so far away when I groan for help?**
**O LORD, do not stay far away!**
**You are my strength; come quickly to my aid!**
**Psalm 22:1, 19**

Psalm 22 is about the suffering, praise and posterity of the Messiah. You can correlate it to the crucifixion and death of Jesus in Matthew 27 and Mark 15. Sometimes we too feel as if the Lord is so far from us. The chaos in our life makes us ask, "Where is God"? That is a human emotion. Jesus being fully human on the cross asked his Father, "Why have you abandoned me?" It is a relevant question to ask our good God because we know he is able to see us through.

Yet later in the text the author says, "You are my strength; come quickly to my aid". While our situation may make it seem like there is no God, our belief that God is real allows us to continue to call on his name. And God answered him because as Jesus breathed his last the curtain in the sanctuary of the Temple was torn in two, from top to bottom.

Jesus gave his life so that we could have full access to the throne room. The Son of God breathed his last breath so that we could breathe forever. At times you may feel abandoned and alone but know that God is always present to hear your cry and rescue you. You need only to cry out to Father and the Lord will take care of you.

***

**Prayer:** *Thank you Father for giving me your only Son, Jesus the Christ. I will run to you in my time of trouble and I will praise you at all times. Thank you for allowing me to go beyond the veil and worship in your presence. I cast all my cares on you, especially those concerning _____*

_____

_____

_____.

*I trust Lord that you will come quickly to my aid.* Amen.

## Let your favor shine on your servant.
## In your unfailing love, rescue me.
## Psalm 31:16

*Lord, in your presence is fullness of joy; at your right hand are pleasures forevermore.* As dreadful and dark as yesterday was, we know the reason. Jesus hung on the cross and said, "It is finished", so we could have eternal life. The greatest thing your heart can experience is God's presence. Because God gave his only Son and because Jesus followed his Father's will, we can experience the fullness of joy in God's presences.

We can experience the Father's favor shining on us. God's unfailing love recues us and delivers us from the hand of our enemies and from those who persecute us. Lord, you alone are God and I thank you for rescuing me.

***

**Prayer:** *God of mercy and favor, thank you for shining on me. Thank you for showering me with your unfailing love. As you love me, let me show love to others. Let my actions represent you as I show mercy and kindness to others especially as it concerns _____*

*_____.*

*I want to hear you say well done. In Jesus name. Amen.*

# Resurrection Sunday

_____ 20 _____

## The stone which the builders rejected has become the chief cornerstone.
### Psalm 118:22 NKJV

This is the day that the Lord has made; let us rejoice and be glad in it. He rose, he rose, he rose from the grave and I am overjoyed about it. This is the Lord's doing and it is marvelous in our eyes. I praise you Lord for the marvelous things that you have done.

My hope is built on nothing less than Jesus' blood and righteousness. I dare not trust the sweetest frame, but wholly lean on Jesus' name. On Christ the solid Rock I stand; all other ground is sinking sand. Jesus rose so that we could live. Praise God for the Chief Cornerstone!

\*\*\*

**TODAY:** *From dusk to dawn, from start to finish, from death to life, from the cross to the throne... Jesus is risen!!!* Jesus rose so that we could live. The journey does not end today. It is just the beginning. Continue to daily practice the spiritual disciplines of prayer, meditation and scripture reading so that you will be equipped to stand against the challenges of the enemy. We wrestle not against flesh and blood, but against powers and rulers of darkness. Stand on the Solid Rock and you will have the victory.

# About the Author

Rev. Joy L. Wilkerson, native of Roxboro, NC, has been a Memphis resident since 1998. She is the proud Pastor of Mt. Herman AME Church in Millington, TN where she was appointed after her ordination as an Itinerant Elder. She previously served as an associate minister at Saint Andrew AME Church. Rev. Joy lives by Philippians 4:6 and truly believes in presenting everything to God with praise and thanksgiving.

Rev. Joy has been spreading the gospel via *The Word* e-mail devotional for over fifteen years. She is passionate about motivating others to move forward and walk worthy of the calling God has for their lives which she exhibited in her first two books: *Deliverance Is Available to You: Motivation to Move Forward* and *Moving Forward: Daily Devotions for the Journey*. Her first book shares her testimony from depression to deliverance. In the fall she will be releasing the sequel to *Deliverance* where she will share her testimony as a single woman dealing with the enemy of distraction.

Rev. Joy has an M.Div. and M.A.R. from Memphis Theological Seminary. She earned her B.S. in Accounting, summa cum laude, from N.C. A & T State University and an MBA from The University of Michigan. She has been published in The A.M.E. Church Review. Rev. Joy is employed as a Data Consultant with a major third party administrator (TPA). She is a proud member of Delta Sigma Theta Sorority, Incorporated. She is the owner of one toy poodle named Jenks.

For more information on Rev. Joy please go to www.mydestaisjoy.com. *About the author* section explains why she uses the name "desta".

Made in the USA
Middletown, DE
18 January 2020